Readers Theatre

Scripted
Rhymes and Rhythms

by Win Braun and Carl Braun

Illustrated by Jeff Reading

PORTAGE & MAIN PRESS

Canadian Cataloguing in Publication Data

Braun, Win, 1959-
  Readers theatre

    ISBN 1-895805-30-9

    1. Readers (Primary)   2. Children's poetry   I. Braun, Carl.
II. Reading, Jeff, 1957- III. Title.
PE1119.B73 1995   428.6   C95-910686-3

Layout design by Henry John Epp

Printed in Canada

PORTAGE & MAIN PRESS

100-318 McDermot Avenue
Winnipeg, Manitoba, Canada, R3A 0A2

Email: books@portageandmainpress.com
Tel: 1-204-987-3500
Toll Free: 1-800-667-9673
Fax: 1-866-734-8477

CONTENTS

For Readers and Groups

ACKNOWLEDGEMENTS

This book has evolved over the years as we have observed children in classrooms and children in less formal settings become involved in chanting rhymes and rhythms. We have seen this happen especially when children were given the opportunity to work together in choral speaking, and particularly in some version of Readers Theatre. Seeing children become hooked for the first time gave us special encouragement to proceed with this book. It always has been especially gratifying to see "turned off" children," so-called reading disabled, and ESL children become actively involved. We thank these children for showing us what should have been obvious to us. We also thank the many teachers and parents who have endorsed Readers Theatre as something that "has a magic about it," something that has the potential to give all children their right to successful and enjoyable learning.

Grateful acknowledgement is also made for permission to reprint the following copyright material: "The Cremation of Sam McGee," by Robert Service; by permission of the Robert Service Estate.

Every effort has been made to trace and acknowledge copyright. However, there are cases in which the publisher was unable to do so. The publisher apologizes for any accidental infringement of copyright and welcomes information that would redress the situation.

READERS THEATRE
AT HOME AND SCHOOL

What is Readers Theatre?

Readers Theatre is a cooperative or shared reading of a poem, story or lyrics of a favourite song. Two or more readers can take part. Even if a piece is scripted for only two readers, and you want more than two readers to participate, assign parts to a duet or chorus. And there are times when you will want to give a part to a weaker and stronger reader for practice, so that one reader supports the other till both feel comfortable enough to read independently. Simple as that. And children love to read cooperatively with older brothers and sisters, parents and teachers, even grandparents.

Readers Theatre requires no memorizing, and no costumes, although at times children may demand costumes. That's fine! Even then, discarded cool shades, hats, shoes, shawls and sashes from the "dress-up" box are more than sufficient. It is important, though, that Readers Theatre be kept simple enough so that you will want to do it often — at bedtime, after school, at any time during the day.

Why Readers Theatre?

It's fun! Even for turned-off readers, it is a **turn-on**. It's fun for the most fluent reader who wants **new challenges**, new channels for her creative energies. It has the potential to generate more enthusiasm and more excitement than most reading activities. What's more, it's fun for parents and teachers.

Readers Theatre is a **supportive** activity. The reader is safe to experiment and take **risks** as **cooperation** rather than competition is valued. If a piece is too difficult the first time around, we simply read along with the reader or allow him to follow a taped reading till he is able to read independently.

Readers Theatre provides more meaningful engagement for all readers than any other reading activity. Whereas weaker readers often become overwhelmed, frequently passive, in more traditional environments, they become **actively involved** in Readers Theatre, often surprising themselves as much as others how well they are able to perform. And built-in **success** is the hallmark of Readers Theatre. Just ask children, teachers and parents who have tried it. As one teacher put it recently, "By mistake I allowed Terry to select a part that I knew was far too difficult for him. I was really worried. I didn't want to discourage him by assigning an easier part, but I also didn't want him to experience failure and discouragement. Well, he came back the next morning with the most enthusiastic, 'I can read my part real good.' And that was an understatement. He must of worked all night at the piece. He just shocked us all by his superb rendition. I was so wrong, so very wrong. I wonder how often I underestimate the abilities of children."

Readers Theatre is one of the best means for children to **learn to hear themselves**, listen to themselves as they try to improve their reading to emulate the best reading they have heard from their parents, teachers or more competent friends. Learning to listen to oneself is one of surest ways for children to improve not only in their reading, but also in their writing. And yes, spelling improves markedly with improved ability to listen to oneself.

Involvement in Readers Theatre is a guarantee for improved **fluent reading**. This is true especially with the use of verse and song. The **rhyme and rhythm** of language enables readers to use larger and larger chunks of print, going beyond the word by word reading that is typical of the weaker reader. And the increasing ability to read with more ease and fluency is one of best guarantees that children will want to spend more time reading.

Readers Theatre invites **celebration** and **performance**. Even the most withdrawn child is moved to **practice**, to listen to herself to see what needs to be improved, and then **practice** some more once she has felt the warmth, support and encouragement that comes from a captive audience. That is likely the **magic** behind Readers Theatre. And the audience may consist of a grandparent, a principal, friends, and for special celebration, the PTA or the school assembly. Even the goal of preparing a piece for taping is enough for many children to keep working on a piece. You will be amazed at the sudden boost to the young reader's **confidence.**

Readers Theatre is for everyone. There isn't a reader anywhere who is unable to participate. The child who is just beginning to follow print, the ESL child, the so-called disabled reader, anyone can work together to produce a Readers Theatre. And that is another benefit. No segregation, no grouping of buzzards and bluebirds. They can all become bluebirds — if we believe in our abilities as parents and teachers, and if we **believe in the creative abilities of our children.**

SUGGESTIONS FOR USE OF THIS BOOK

Once you start working with Readers Theatre, you really won't need anyone to suggest what to do. You will come up with many ways of adding interest and variation to the readings. We simply offer a few suggestions to help you get started.

1. Aim to make all reading free of stress. If a child is reluctant or fearful, read his part with him giving only as much support as necessary. Some groups will benefit from reading the entire piece in chorus as a "warm up," and then move into reading in parts.

2. Some children, especially those children who have already experienced difficulty in read-

ing, will do well to have a taped version of the entire piece as a resource. A child may read along through an entire piece, or simply check to see how her own part is read. For many this is a kind of security blanket till they become comfortable with Readers Theatre and till they discover that they are capable of more than they thought.

3 As an "at home" activity, many of the pieces will suggest more parts than the number of children available. No problem! One person can take a chorus part; one person (often an adult) can be assigned to read the parts of two readers. Or larger chunks of the piece can be read by two or three people in the form of chorus reading.

4. Encourage children to be on the lookout for poetry or song lyrics that they can script for Readers Theatre. Scripting a piece makes a wonderful group or individual writing activity. And what a boost to children's ability to listen to their own reading as they refine their scripts. And improved listening, again, is going to mean a boost to their writing.

5 Encourage children to experiment with their voices as they read. Record their renditions and encourage them to talk about what they like about their reading, and what they want to change in future readings.

6. Make Readers Theatre a significant part of your home and school reading program. Give it high profile, including children's own scripts and tapes of their renditions (including pieces done at home) as part of their portfolios. You will find that even some of the more dramatic nursery rhymes, the Shel Silverstein or Dennis Lee poetry, or "The Night Before Christmas," take on new life.

7. To involve the whole class, use the overhead projector. Assign groups of children to be each part. This is a way of providing a safe environment for children to learn the various parts in a script and for them to get ideas for using voices to portray a character, etc. Here are some suggested scripts: *The Freight Train, Little Gray Mouse, The Backyard Fuss, Down By the Bay, Boing!Boing!Boing!, The Daddy Long-Legs and the Fly, Silly Billy Goats* and *Mr. Finney's Turnip.*

8. We highly recommend that you encourage children to read some of the earlier published, colour-illustrated versions of some of the pieces in this book. For example, check out the wonderfully illustrated book by Ted Harrison of *The Cremation of Sam McGee,* Ezra Jack Keats' illustrated version of *Over in the Meadow* or some of the beautiful versions of Edward Lear's *The Owl and the Pussy-Cat* (an especially appealing version illustrated by Jan Brett, G. P. Putnam's, 1991) It is very encouraging for children to discover that they are able to read independently what they have read as a Readers Theatre piece earlier. And they find that it's fun.

9. Keep enjoyment at the forefront.

ANIMAL NONSENSE RHYMES

by Mabel F. Hill

Reader 1:   The skunk is never without a scent,
So he can always pay his rent.

Reader 2:   The turtle's house is on his back;
No rent to pay. No clothes to pack.

Reader 3:   The elephant's trunk is always there
If he wants to travel anywhere.

Reader 1:   The 'possum and the kangaroo
Have pockets to carry their treasures too.

Reader 2:   The clam and oyster and the snail
Have a little house like a coat of mail.

Rooster: I'm always neat

Reader 3:   The rooster said,

Rooster: I keep a comb fast to my head.

Reader 1:   The rabbit's tail is his powder puff,
He likes to live on garden stuff,

Reader 2:   The spider spins a web-like trap,
Then settles down to take a nap.

THE BARNYARD FUSS

by Helen Kitchell Evans

Reader 1:   Out in the barnyard at half-past two
The lavender cow went

Chorus: **Moo-moo-moo.**

Reader 2:   The big yellow dog set up a yow
He barked and he barked,

Chorus: **Bow-wow, bow-wow.**

Reader 1:   The big red rooster joined in it, too
With his

Chorus: **Cock-a-doodle, doodle-do.**

Readers Theatre: Scripted Rhymes and Rhythms

Reader 2: The cat on the fence was in a stew
And she began with a

Chorus: Mew-mew-mew.

Reader 1: The spotted pig didn't want to be left out
So he called

Chorus: Wee-wee, wee-wee.

Reader 2: The fat old duck with his rainproof back
Started to sing his

Chorus: Quack, quack, quack.

Reader 1: All of this noise brought the farmer out
To see what the terrible fuss was about.

Reader 2: He laughed and he laughed at what he saw
With a

Chorus: Hee-haw, hee-haw, hee-haw-haw.

Reader 1: For there was the little brown hen
Right in a puddle of mud
Clear up to her chin!

Reader 2: And loudly she cried,
Get me out of this muck!

Chorus: *Cluckity, cluckity, cluckity, cluck!*

Anonymous

Reader 1: "Moo," says the cow,

All: I like hay.

Reader 2: "Bow-woo," says the dog,

All: Bones, any day!

Reader 3: "Milk," says kitty cat,

All: And nice fresh fish.

Reader 1: "I," said the bee,

All: Sip honey where I wish.

Reader 2: "Quack," says the duck,

All: Corn is best of all.

Reader 3: "Mice are really nicer,"

All: Says the Owl on the wall.

Reader 1: Baby says,

All: "A-goo, a-goo;
I like bread and milk, I do!"

THE LITTLE GRAY MOUSE

by Rawley Lemley

Reader 1: Dickery, dockery, little gray mouse;
Reader 2: Back in the cupboard,
Reader 3: All over the house.

Reader 1: Hickery, dickery, go where you please!
Reader 2: Sniffing and snuffing,
Reader 3: Searching for cheese.

Reader 1: Squeakery, sneakery, slipping about!
Reader 2: Haste to the pantry!
Reader 3: Everyone's out.

Reader 1: Creeping and peeking, like a wee elf;
Reader 2: Nibbling the cookies
Reader 3: Up on the shelf.

Reader 1: Playing and straying, Hark! What was that?
Reader 2: Scurry and flurry!
All: Here comes the **CAT**!

FIVE CANTANKEROUS CROCODILES

by Carl Braun

Reader 1:	**Five** cantankerous crocodiles
Reader 2:	In a thunderous downpour;
Reader 3:	One lost his umbrella,
All:	And that left **four**.

Reader 1:	**Four** cantankerous crocodiles
Reader 2:	Slith'ring about in glee;
Reader 3:	One swam away,
All:	And that left **three**.

Reader 1:	**Three** cantankerous crocodiles
Reader 2:	Scaring the fishes, **BOO!**
Reader 3:	One lost his way,
All:	And that left **two**.

Reader 1:	**Two** cantankerous crocodiles
Reader 2:	Heard a far-off gun;
Reader 3:	One ducked underwater,
All:	And that left **one**.

Reader 1:	**One** cantankerous crocodile
Reader 2:	Eyes gleaming with a **TEAR-O!**
Reader 3:	Sadly slithered down the stream,
All:	And that left **zero**.

Readers Theatre: Scripted Rhymes and Rhythms &Braun Braun ©

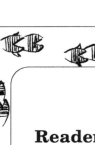

FIVE LITTLE PIGGIES

by Carl Braun

Reader 1:   Five little piggies waiting to be fed,

Reader 2:   The first little piggie said,

Chorus: Give me milk and bread!

Reader 1:   The second little piggie said,

Chorus: I like corn and peas,

Reader 2:   The third little piggie said,

Chorus: Peas make me sneeze!

Reader 1:   The fourth little piggie said,

Chorus: I like pumpkin pies,

Reader 2:   The fifth little piggie said,

Chorus: Pies in pig styes?

Reader 1:   Farmer Jones just took one look

Reader 2:   at the five hungry eyes,

Reader 1:   He grabbed a bucket fit for five

All: and dumped a load of fries!

FIVE LITTLE SQUIRRELS

Traditional

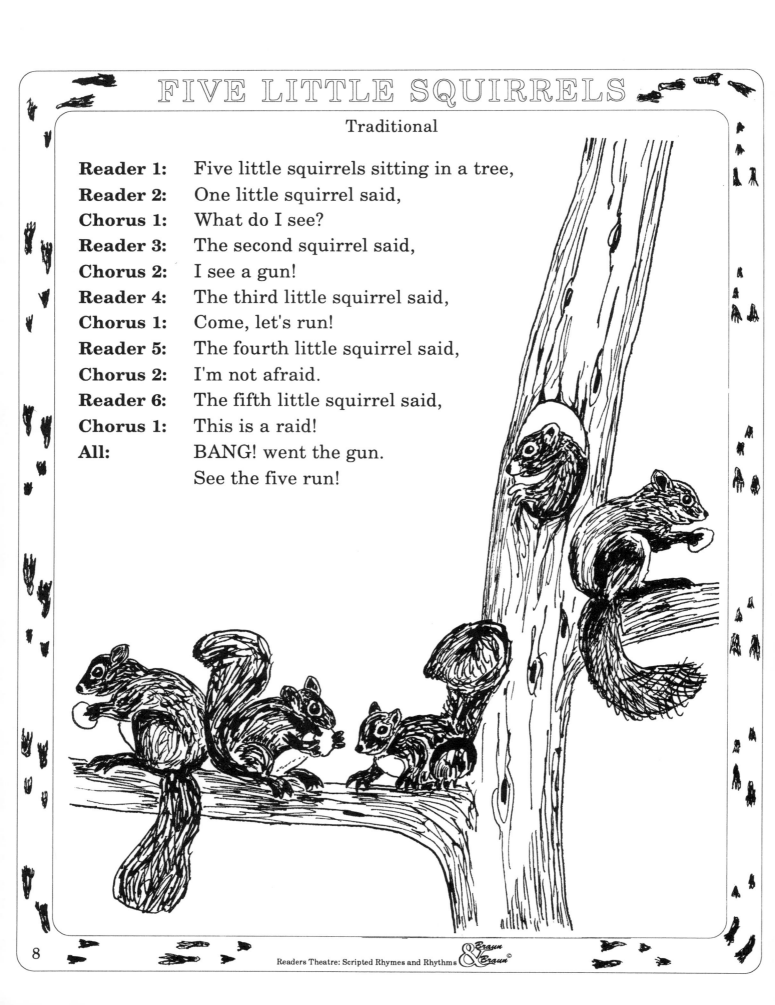

Reader 1: Five little squirrels sitting in a tree,

Reader 2: One little squirrel said,

Chorus 1: What do I see?

Reader 3: The second squirrel said,

Chorus 2: I see a gun!

Reader 4: The third little squirrel said,

Chorus 1: Come, let's run!

Reader 5: The fourth little squirrel said,

Chorus 2: I'm not afraid.

Reader 6: The fifth little squirrel said,

Chorus 1: This is a raid!

All: BANG! went the gun.
See the five run!

Readers Theatre: Scripted Rhymes and Rhythms Braun &Braun ©

ARE YOU A GOLLY-WOCK

Anonymous

Reader 1: A Golly-wock is someone
Who is very impolite.

Reader 2: He never says. **"Good Morning,"**

Reader 3: And he never says **"Good Night."**

Reader 1: He never thinks of **"Thank you,"**

Reader 2: And he never says **"Please."**

Reader 3: You'd never think he'd ever heard
About words so nice as these.

Reader 1: If you should ever meet him,
Does he call a big **"Hello,"**

Reader 2: Or say **"I beg your pardon"**
If he steps upon your toe.

Reader 3: Oh, no! he always mumbles

Reader 1: And pretends he doesn't care.

Reader 2: He never says **"I'm sorry"**
To a person anywhere.

Reader 3: He never hangs his coat up,

Reader 1: He never puts away his toys.

Reader 2: He never gets his hands clean
Like other girls and boys.

Reader 3: He's always most unhappy,

Reader 1: And he's very lonesome, too;

Reader 2: A Golly-Wock is someone
That I wouldn't be!

All: **Would you?**

Braun & Braun © Readers Theatre: Scripted Rhymes and Rhythms   9

BOING! BOING! SQUEAK!

by Jack Prelutsky

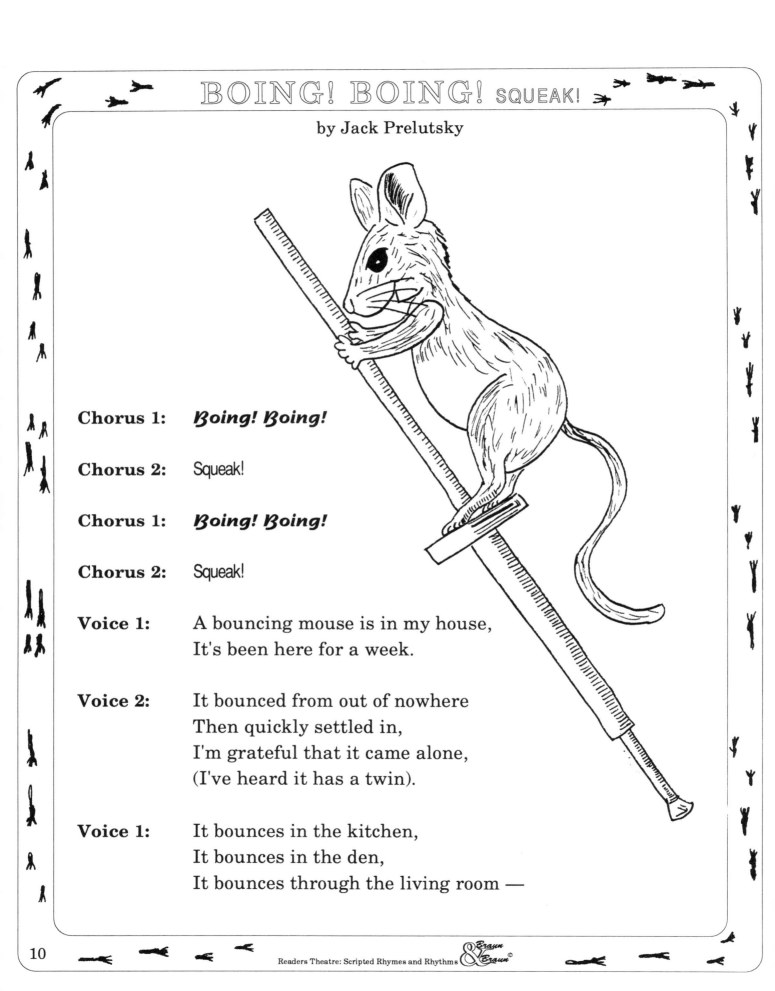

Chorus 1: *Boing! Boing!*

Chorus 2: Squeak!

Chorus 1: *Boing! Boing!*

Chorus 2: Squeak!

Voice 1: A bouncing mouse is in my house,
It's been here for a week.

Voice 2: It bounced from out of nowhere
Then quickly settled in,
I'm grateful that it came alone,
(I've heard it has a twin).

Voice 1: It bounces in the kitchen,
It bounces in the den,
It bounces through the living room —

Voice 2:   LOOK! There it goes again.

Chorus 1:   *Boing! Boing!*

Chorus 2:   Squeak!

Chorus 1:   *Boing! Boing!*

Chorus 2:   Squeak!

Voice 1:   A bouncing mouse is in my house,
It's been here for a week.

Voice 2:   It bounces on the sofa,
On the table and the bed,
Up the stairs and on the chairs,
And even on my head.

Voice 1:   That mouse continues bouncing
Every minute of the day,
It bounces, bounces, bounces,
But it doesn't bounce away.

Chorus 1:   *Boing! Boing!*

Chorus 2:   Squeak!

Voice 1:   A bouncing mouse is in my house,

Voice 2:   It's been here for a week.

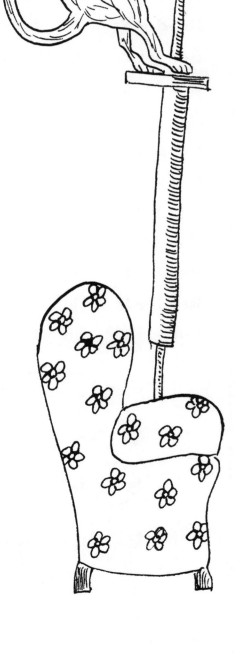

IN THE BARBER SHOP

by Bernard Hirshberg

Reader 1:   Snip.

Reader 2:   Snap,

Reader 3:   Snappity,

Voices: SNIP!

Reader 1:   Down goes my hair!

Reader 2:   Oh, Mister Barber,

Reader 3:   STOP THAT CLIP,

Reader 1:   Before my head is bare!

Reader 2:   Snip.

Reader 3:   Snap,

Reader 1:   Snappity

Voices: WHIRL!

Reader 2:   What a falling chain!

Reader 3:   Don't you worry little girl,

Voices: They'll grow back again.

Readers Theatre: Scripted Rhymes and Rhythms

CHANT

by David McCord

Reader 1: The cow has a cud
The turtle has mud
Reader 2: The rabbit has a hutch
But I haven't much

Reader 3: The ox has a yoke
The frog has a croak
Reader 4: The toad has a wart
So he's not my sort

Reader 1: The mouse has a hole
The polecat a pole
Reader 2: The goose has a hiss
And it goes like this

Reader 3: The duck has a pond
The bird has beyond
Reader 4: The hen has a chick
But I feel sick

All: The crow has a nest
The hawk has a quest
The owl has a mate
Doggone! I'm late!

THE FREIGHT TRAIN

by Nona Keen Duffy

All: **Choo-choo! Puff-puff!**
             Pull, pull, pull!

Group 1: I can carry many things
             When all my cars are full!

All: **Toot-toot! Puff-puff!**
             Roll, roll, roll!

Group 2: The engineer has pulled a cord,
             The fireman shovels coal!

All: **Rumble-rumble! Rumble-rumble!**
             Ding-ding-dong!

Group 3: Hear me grumble, hear me mumble
             As I roll along!

All: **Choo-choo! Puff-puff!**
             Roll, roll, roll!

Group 4: Box cars for furniture
             Coal cars for coal!

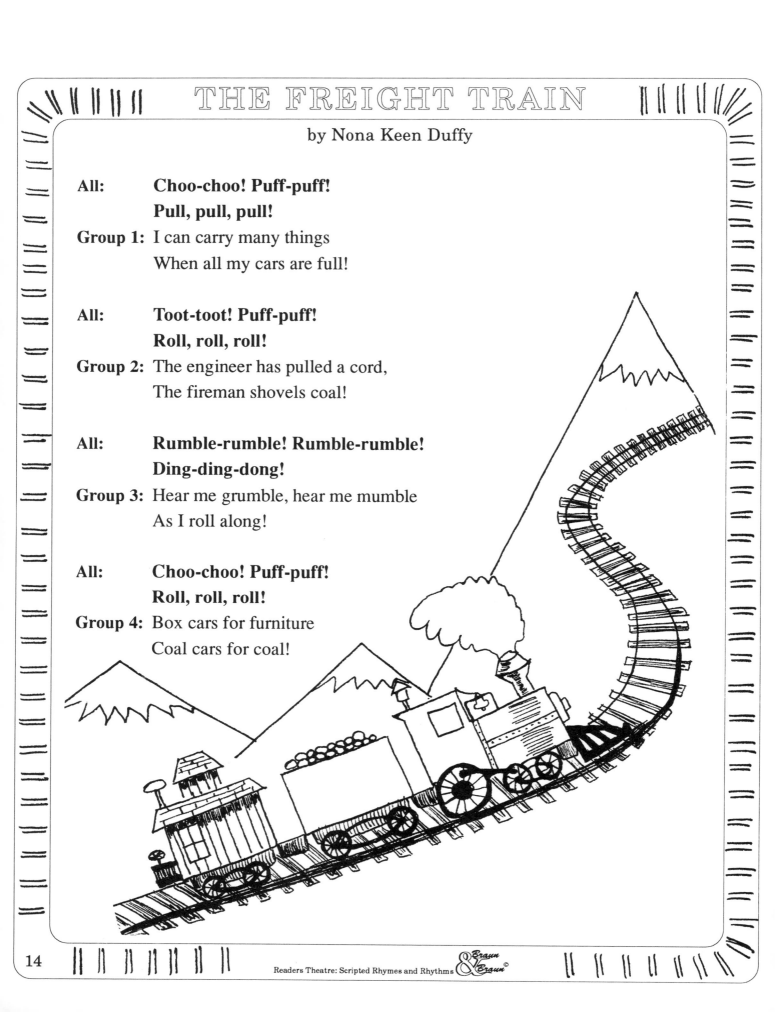

Readers Theatre: Scripted Rhymes and Rhythms

Group 1: Tank cars for gasoline,
Long and slick and black;

Group 2: Flat cars and auto cars
Rumble down the track!

Group 3: Box cars for oranges,
Apples, dates and wheat,

Group 4: Turkeys, beef and mutton chops
And many things to eat!

All: **Puff, puff! Puff, puff!**

Group 1: See my white steam blowing,

All: **Clang, clang! Toot, toot!**

Group 2: Down the track I'm going!

All: **Choo, choo! Ding, dong!**
Pull, pull, pull!

Group 3: I've a thousand things for you,

Group 4: For all my cars are full!

ONE, TWO, THREE!

by Henry Cuyler Bunner

Reader 1:   It was an old, old, old, old lady,

Reader 2:   And a boy who was half past three;

Reader 3:   And the way they played together

Reader 4:   Was beautiful to see.

Reader 1:   She couldn't go romping and jumping,

Reader 2:   And the boy no more could he;

Reader 3:   For he was a thin little fellow,

Reader 4:   With a thin little twisted knee.

Reader 1:   They sat in the yellow sunlight,

Reader 2:   Out under the maple tree;

Reader 3:   And the game they played I'll tell you,

Just as it was told to me.

Reader 4:   It was hide-and-go-seek they were playing,

Reader 1:   Though you'd never have known it to be —

Reader 2:   With an old, old, old, old lady,

Reader 3:   And a boy with a twisted knee.

Reader 4:   The boy would bend his face down

Reader 1:   On his little sound right knee,

Reader 2:   And he guessed where she was hiding

Reader 3:   In guesses One,

Reader 4:   Two,

Reader 1:   Three.

Readers Theatre: Scripted Rhymes and Rhythms Braun & Braun ©

Reader 2:	"You are in the china closet!"
Reader 3:	He would laugh and cry with glee —
Reader 4:	It wasn't the china closet,
Reader 1:	But he still had Two
Reader 3:	and Three.

Reader 2:	"You are up in Papa's big bedroom,
	In the chest with the queer old key!"
Reader 4:	And she said,
Reader 1:	"You are warm and warmer,
	But you're not quite right,"
Reader 3:	said she.

Reader 2:	"It can't be the little cupboard
	Where Mamma's things used to be —
	So it must be in the clothespress, Gran'ma,"
Reader 4:	And he found her with his Three.

Reader 1:	Then she covered her face with her fingers,
Reader 2:	That was wrinkled and white and wee,
Reader 3:	And she guessed where the boy was hiding,
Reader 4:	With a One
Reader 1:	and a Two
Reader 2:	and a Three.

Reader 3:	And they never had stirred from their places,
Reader 4:	Right under the maple tree —
Reader 1:	This old, old, old, old lady,
Reader 2:	And the boy with the lame little knee —
Reader 3:	This dear, dear, dear old lady,
Reader 4:	And the boy who was half past three.

THE CREMATION OF SAM McGEE

by Robert Service

Reader 1:   There are strange things done in the midnight sun
By the men who moil for gold;
The Arctic trails have their secret tales
That would make your blood run cold;

Reader 2:   The Northern Lights have seen queer sights,
But the queerest they ever did see
Was that night on the marge of Lake Lebarge
I cremated Sam McGee.

Reader 3:   Now Sam McGee was from Tennessee,
where the cotton blooms and blows.
Why he left his home in the South to roam
'round the Pole, God only knows.

Reader 4:   He was always cold, but the land of gold
seemed to hold him like a spell;
Though he'd often say in his homely way
that "he'd sooner live in hell."

Braun & Braun©

Reader 1:   On a Christmas Day we were mushing our way
over the Dawson trail.
Talk of your cold! through the parka's fold
it stabbed like a driven nail.

Reader 2:   If our eyes we'd close, then the lashes froze
till sometimes we couldn't see;
It wasn't much fun, but the only one
to whimper was Sam McGee.

Reader 3:   And that very night, as we lay packed tight
in our robes beneath the snow,
And the dogs were fed, and the stars o'erhead
were dancing heel to toe,

Reader 4:   He turned to me, and

Sam McGee: Cap

Reader 4:   says he,

Sam McGee: I'll cash in this trip, I guess;
And if I do, I'm asking that you
won't refuse my last request.

Reader 1:   Well, he seemed so low that I couldn't say no;
then he says with a sort of moan:

Sam McGee: It's the cursed cold, and it's got right hold
till I'm chilled clean through to the bone.
Yet 'tain't being dead — it's my awful dread
of the icy grave that pains;
So I want you to swear that, foul or fair,
you'll cremate my last remains.

Reader 2:   A pal's last need is a thing to heed,
so I swore I would not fail;
And we started on at the streak of dawn;
but God! he looked ghastly pale.

Reader 3:   He crouched on the sleigh, and he raved all day
of his home in Tennessee;
And before nightfall a corpse was all
that was left of Sam McGee.

Reader 4:   There wasn't a breath in that land of death,
and I hurried, horror-driven,
With a corpse half hid that I couldn't get rid,
because of a promise given.

Reader 1:   It was lashed to the sleigh, and it seemed to say:

Sam McGee: You may tax your brawn and brains,
But you promised true, and it's up to you
to cremate those last remains.

Braun & Braun ©

Reader 2: Now a promise made is a debt unpaid,
and the trail has its own stern code.
In the days to come, though my lips were dumb,
in my heart how I cursed that load.

Reader 3: In the long, long night, by the lone firelight,
while the huskies, round in a ring,
Howled out their woes to the homeless snows —
O God! how I loathed the thing.

Reader 4: And every day that quiet clay
seemed to heavy and heavier grow;
And on I went, though the dogs were spent
and the grub was getting low;

Reader 1: The trail was bad, and I felt half mad,
but I swore I would not give in;
And I'd often sing to the hateful thing,
and it hearkened with a grin.

Reader 2: Till I came to the marge of Lake Lebarge,
and a derelict there lay;
It was jammed in the ice, but I saw in a trice
it was called the "Alice May."

Reader 3: And I looked at it, and I thought a bit,
and I looked at my frozen chum;
Then "Here," said I, with a sudden cry,
"is my cre-ma-tor-eum."

Reader 4:   Some planks I tore from the cabin floor,
                 and I lit the boiler fire;
                 Some coal I found that was lying around,
                 and I heaped the fuel higher;

Reader 1:   The flames just soared, and the furnace roared —
                 such a blaze you seldom see;
                 And I burrowed a hole in the glowing coal,
                 and I stuffed in Sam McGee.

Reader 2:   Then I made a hike, for I didn't like
                 to hear him sizzle so;
                 And the heavens scowled, and the huskies howled,
                 and the wind began to blow.

Reader 3:   It was icy cold, but the hot sweat rolled
                 down my cheeks, and I don't know why;
                 And the greasy smoke in an inky cloak
                 went streaking down the sky.

Reader 4:   I do not know how long in the snow

I wrestled with grisly fear;

But the stars came out and they danced about

ere again I ventured near;

Reader 1:   I was sick with dread, but I bravely said;

"I'll just take a peep inside.

I guess he's cooked, and it's time I looked";

...then the door I opened wide.

Reader 2:   And there sat Sam, looking cool and calm,

in the heart of the furnace roar;

And he wore a smile you could see a mile,

and he said:

Sam McGee: Please close that door.

It's fine in here, but I greatly fear

you'll let in the cold and storm —

Since I left Plumtree, down in Tennessee,

it's the first time I've been warm."

Reader 3:   There are strange things done in the midnight sun

By the men who moil for gold;

The Arctic trails have their secret tales

That would make your blood run cold;

Reader 4:   The Northern Lights have seen queer sights,

But the queerest they ever did see

Was that night on the marge of Lake Lebarge

I cremated Sam McGee.

CASEY AT THE BAT

by Ernest Lawrence Thayer

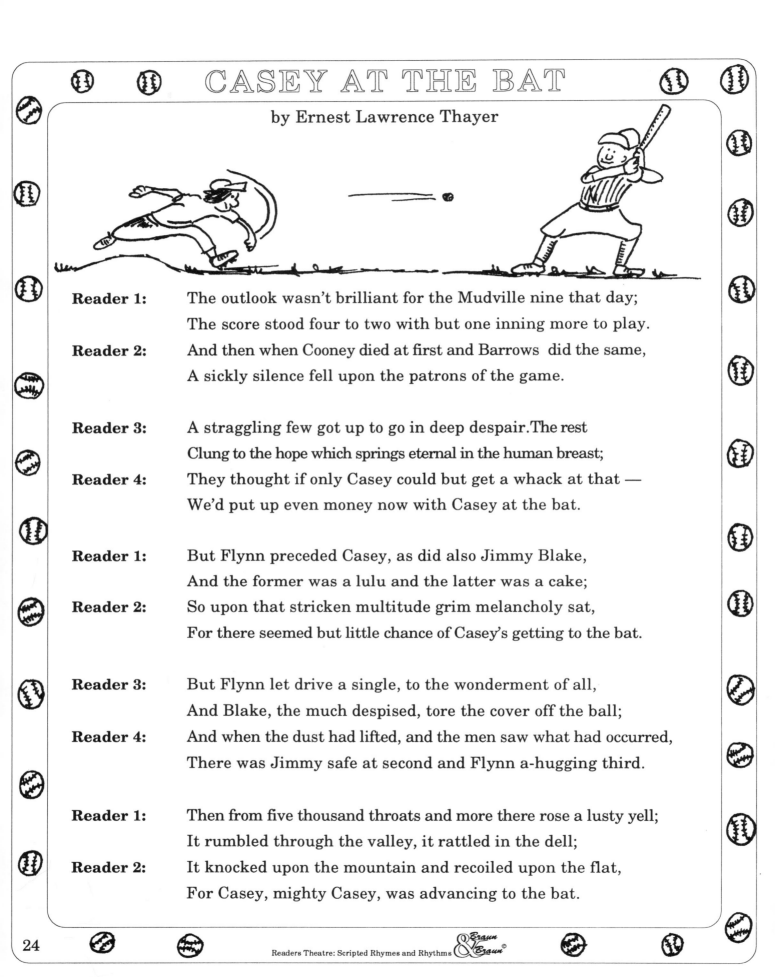

Reader 1: The outlook wasn't brilliant for the Mudville nine that day;
The score stood four to two with but one inning more to play.

Reader 2: And then when Cooney died at first and Barrows did the same,
A sickly silence fell upon the patrons of the game.

Reader 3: A straggling few got up to go in deep despair. The rest
Clung to the hope which springs eternal in the human breast;

Reader 4: They thought if only Casey could but get a whack at that —
We'd put up even money now with Casey at the bat.

Reader 1: But Flynn preceded Casey, as did also Jimmy Blake,
And the former was a lulu and the latter was a cake;

Reader 2: So upon that stricken multitude grim melancholy sat,
For there seemed but little chance of Casey's getting to the bat.

Reader 3: But Flynn let drive a single, to the wonderment of all,
And Blake, the much despised, tore the cover off the ball;

Reader 4: And when the dust had lifted, and the men saw what had occurred,
There was Jimmy safe at second and Flynn a-hugging third.

Reader 1: Then from five thousand throats and more there rose a lusty yell;
It rumbled through the valley, it rattled in the dell;

Reader 2: It knocked upon the mountain and recoiled upon the flat,
For Casey, mighty Casey, was advancing to the bat.

Readers Theatre: Scripted Rhymes and Rhythms

Reader 3: There was ease in Casey's manner as he stepped into his place;
There was pride in Casey's bearing and a smile on Casey's face.

Reader 4: And when, responding to the cheers, he lightly doffed his hat,
No stranger in the crowd could doubt 'twas Casey at the bat.

Reader 1: Ten thousand eyes were on him as he rubbed his hands with dirt;
Five thousand tongues applauded when he wiped them on his shirt.

Reader 2: Then while the writhing pitcher ground the ball into his hip,
Defiance gleamed in Casey's eye, a sneer curled Casey's lip.

Reader 3: And now the leather-covered sphere came hurtling through the air,
And Casey stood a-watching it in haughty grandeur there.

Reader 4: Close by the sturdy batsman the ball unheeded sped —
"That ain't my style," said Casey. "Strike one," the umpire said.

Reader 1: From the benches, black with people, there went up a muffled roar,
Like the beating of the storm waves on a stern and distant shore.

Reader 2: "Kill him! Kill the umpire!" shouted someone on the stand;
And it's likely they'd have killed him had not Casey raised his hand.

Reader 3: With a smile of Christian charity great Casey's visage shone;
He stilled the rising tumult; he bade the game go on;

Reader 4: He signalled to the pitcher, and once more the spheroid flew;
But Casey still ignored it, and the umpire said, "Strike two."

Reader 1: "Fraud!" cried the maddened thousands, and echo answered, "Fraud!"
But one scornful look from Casey and the audience was awed.

Reader 2: They saw his face grow stern and cold, they saw his muscles strain,
And they knew that Casey wouldn't let that ball go by again.

Reader 3: The sneer is gone from Casey's lip, his teeth are clenched in hate;
He pounds with cruel violence his bat upon the plate.

Reader 4: And now the pitcher holds the ball, and now he lets it go,
And now the air is shattered by the force of Casey's blow.

Reader 1: Oh, somewhere in this favoured land the sun is shining bright;
The band is playing somewhere, and somewhere hearts are light,

Reader 2: And somewhere men are laughing, and somewhere children shout;
But there is no joy in Mudville — mighty Casey has struck out.

by Ilo Orleans

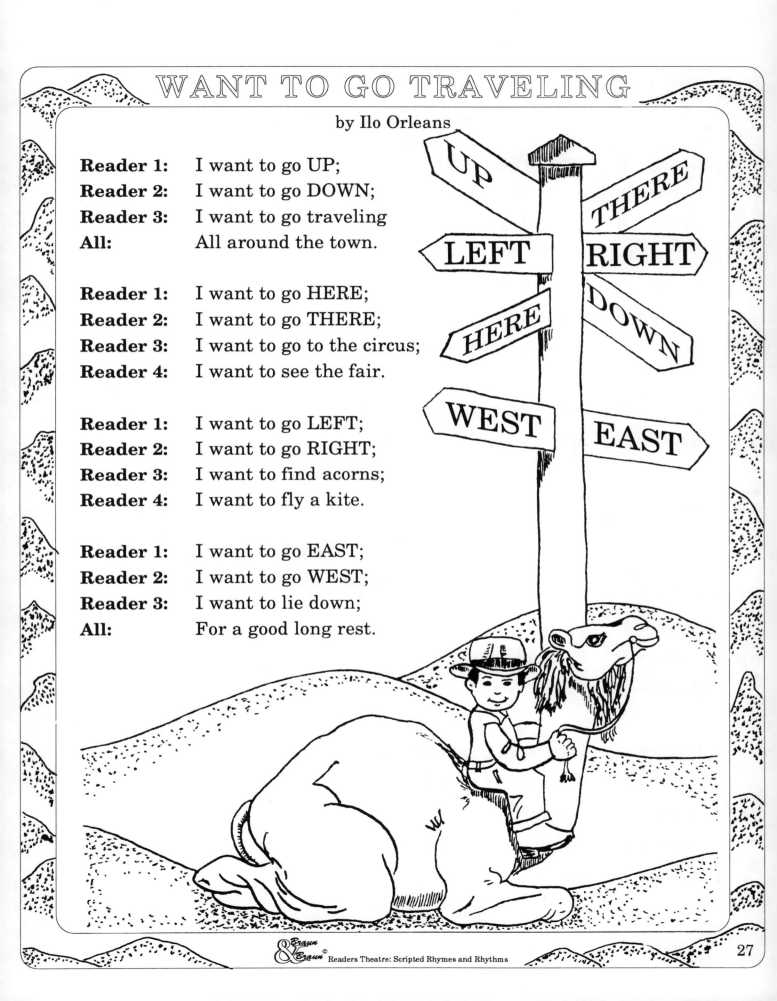

Reader 1:   I want to go UP;
Reader 2:   I want to go DOWN;
Reader 3:   I want to go traveling
All: All around the town.

Reader 1:   I want to go HERE;
Reader 2:   I want to go THERE;
Reader 3:   I want to go to the circus;
Reader 4:   I want to see the fair.

Reader 1:   I want to go LEFT;
Reader 2:   I want to go RIGHT;
Reader 3:   I want to find acorns;
Reader 4:   I want to fly a kite.

Reader 1:   I want to go EAST;
Reader 2:   I want to go WEST;
Reader 3:   I want to lie down;
All: For a good long rest.

PETER RABBIT

by W. L. Simpkins

Reader 1:   Small Peter Rabbit

Reader 2:   Had a bad habit:

Reader 3:   He couldn't let lettuce alone.

Reader 1:   He told all his brothers

Reader 2:   And they told still others

Reader 3:   Of a garden where lettuce had grown.

Reader 1:   So there they came creeping,

Reader 2:   All peeping and creeping,

Reader 3:   In night-time and day-time,

Reader 1:   In rain and in dew.

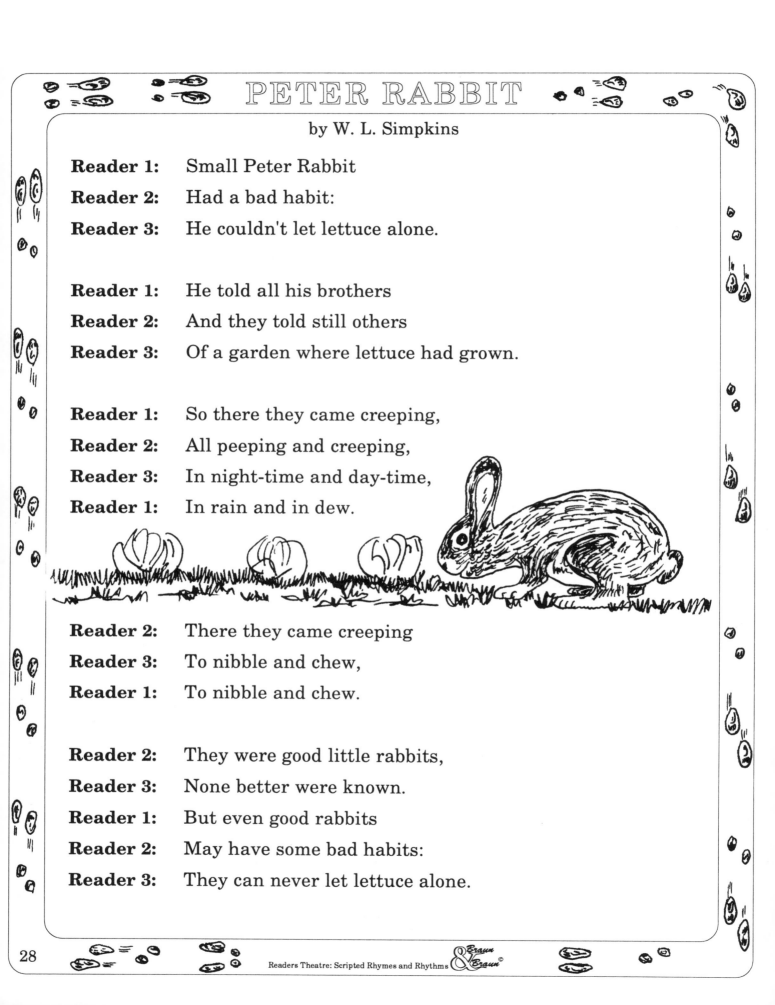

Reader 2:   There they came creeping

Reader 3:   To nibble and chew,

Reader 1:   To nibble and chew.

Reader 2:   They were good little rabbits,

Reader 3:   None better were known.

Reader 1:   But even good rabbits

Reader 2:   May have some bad habits:

Reader 3:   They can never let lettuce alone.

Readers Theatre: Scripted Rhymes and Rhythms &Braun &Braun©

DOWN BY THE BAY

Traditional

Chorus: Down by the bay
Where the watermelons grow
Back to my home
I dare not go.

Reader 1: For if I do, my mother will say,
Mother: "Did you ever see a moose
With its front tooth loose?"
Reader 2: Down by the bay.

Chorus: Down by the bay
Where the watermelons grow
Back to my home
I dare not go.

Reader 1: For if I do, my mother will say,
Mother: "Did you ever see a cow
With a green eyebrow?"
Reader 2: Down by the bay.

THE TWO OLD BACHELORS

by Edward Lear

Reader 1:   Two old bachelors were living in one house;

Reader 2:   One caught a Muffin,

Reader 3:   The other caught a Mouse.

Reader 1:   Said he who caught the Muffin

Reader 2:   to him who caught the Mouse —

Bachelor 1:   This happens just in time!
For we've nothing in the house.
Save a tiny slice of lemon,
and a teaspoonful of honey,

Bachelor 2:   And what to do for dinner —
since we haven't any money?

Bachelor 1:   And what can we expect,
if we haven't any dinner,
But to lose our teeth and eyelashes
and keep on growing thinner?

Reader 3:   Said he who caught the Mouse

Reader 1:   to him who caught the Muffin —

Readers Theatre: Scripted Rhymes and Rhythms   Braun &Braun ©

Bachelor 2: We might cook this little Mouse,
if we only had some Stuffin'!
If we had but Sage and Onion
we could do extremely well,
But how to get that Stuffin'
it is difficult to tell!

Reader 2: Those two old Bachelors
ran quickly to the town
And asked for Sage and Onion
as they wandered up and down.

Reader 3: They borrowed two large Onions,
but no Sage was to be found
In the Shops, or in the Market,
or in all the Gardens round.

Reader 1:   But someone said, —

Reader 2:   A hill there is, a little to the north,
And to its purpledicular top a narrow way leads forth; —
And there among the rugged rocks abides an ancient Sage, —

Reader 3:   An earnest Man, who reads all day a most perplexing page.
Climb up, and seize him by the toes! — all studious as he sits —

Reader 1:   And pull him down — and chop him into endless little bits!

Reader 2:   Then mix him with your Onion (cut lengthwise into Scraps) —
Then your Stuffin' will be ready — and very good: perhaps.

Reader 3:   Those two old bachelors without loss of time
The nearly purpledicular crags at once began to climb;

Reader 1:   And at the top, among the rocks, all seated in a nook,
They saw that Sage, a-reading of a most enormous book.

Bachelor 1 & 2:   You earnest Sage!

Reader 2:   aloud they cried,

Bachelor 1 & 2:   Your book you've read enough in! —
We wish to chop you into bits to mix you into Stuffin'!

Reader 3:   But that old Sage looked calmly up,
and with his awful book,
At those two Bachelors' bald heads
a certain aim he took.

Reader 1: And over crag and precipice
they rolled promiscuous down, —
At once they rolled, and never stopped
in lane or field or town.

Reader 2: And when they reached their house,
they found (besides their want of Stuffin'),
The Mouse had fled — and,
previously, had eaten up the Muffin.

Reader 3: They left their home in silence
by the once convivial door,

Reader 1: And from that hour those Bachelors
were never heard of more.

GOLDILOCKS, GOLDILOCKS

by Carl Braun

Group 1:   Goldilocks, Goldilocks, where are you going?

Goldilocks: For a stroll in the woods, where flowers are growing.

Group 2:   Goldilocks, Goldilocks, what do you see?

Goldilocks: I see a cottage beckoning me.

Group 1:   Goldilocks, Goldilocks, is someone inside?

Goldilocks: I'll take a peek, then run and hide.

Group 2:   Goldilocks, Goldilocks, what do you see?

Goldilocks: Three bowls of porridge staring at me.
              One hot, one cold,
              One right to a tee.

Group 1:   Goldilocks, Goldilocks, what will you do?

Goldilocks: I'll eat the one, and leave the two.

Group 2:   Goldilocks, Goldilocks, what do you see?

Goldilocks: A chair that's hard,
              And one that's soft,
              And one exactly right for me.

Readers Theatre: Scripted Rhymes and Rhythms

Group 1:	Goldilocks, Goldilocks, what have you done?
Goldilocks:	I've accidentally wrecked the little one.

Group 2:	Goldilocks, Goldilocks, how do you feel?
Goldilocks:	A little woozy after that meal.

Group 1:	Goldilocks, Goldilocks, what do you see?
Goldilocks:	A bed that's hard,
	And one that's soft,
	And one exactly right for me.

Group 2:	Goldilocks, Goldilocks, I hear you snore,
	If you'd see what I see, you'd head for the door.

Group 1:	Goldilocks, Goldilocks, what do you see?
Goldilocks:	Six beary eyes glowering at me.

Group 2:	Goldilocks, Goldilocks, though you're so bold,
Group 1:	You've been trespassing, take to the road.

Group 2:	Goldilocks, Goldilocks, now what do you say?
Goldilocks:	I was a fool to come this way!

LITTLE RED RIDING HOOD

by Carl Braun

Group 1: Little Red Riding Hood, what do you see?
Little Red: A basket of goodies for Grandma's tea.

Group 2: Little Red Riding Hood, what did Mom say?
Little Red: Whatever you do, don't stop on the way.

Group 1: Little Red Riding Hood, who's talking to you?
Little Red: Just a friendly old wolf, no big to do.

Group 2: Little Red Riding Hood, what did he say?
Little Red: See you later, have a good day.

Group 1: Little Red Riding Hood, what do you see?
Little Red: A bunch of flowers for Granny and me.

Group 2: Little Red Riding Hood, what's your plan?
Little Red: I'm on my way now as fast as I can.

Readers Theatre: Scripted Rhymes and Rhythms   Braun &Braun©

Group 1:   Little Red Riding Hood, don't go inside,
Group 2:   There's a hairy creature, his mouth open wide.

Group 1:   Little Red Riding Hood, what do you see?
Little Red: Two ears that have stretched, good gracious me!

Group 2:   Little Red Riding Hood, what do you think?
Little Red: There's something strange about Granny's wink.

Group 1:   Little Red Riding Hood, how do you feel?
Little Red: Granny's not well, no big deal!

Group 2:   Little Red Riding Hood, please head for the door.
Group 1:   That bed-ridden creature will charge on all four.

Group 2:   Little Red Riding Hood, what will you do?
Little Red: I think I can expect the woodsmen crew.

Group 1:   Little Red Riding Hood, how did you know?
Little Red: This story's on every children's show.

SILLY BILLY GOATS

by Carl Braun

Reader 1:   Billy Goats, Billy Goats, what do you see?

3 Goats: A hill with green grass, just right for us three.

Reader 2:   Billy Goats, Billy Goats, what will you do?

3 Goats: We'll cross that bridge, there's grass to chew.

Reader 1:   Billy Goats, Billy Goats, what do you see?

3 Goats: An ugly old troll, no match for us three!

Reader 2:   Little old troll, little old troll, what do you hear?

Troll: A trip-trip-trapping coming near.

Reader 1:   Little old troll, little old troll, what will you do?

Troll: I'm going to make some lovely goat stew.

Reader 2:   Billy Goat One, now what do you hear?

Goat 1:   An ugly old troll is threatening me.

Reader 1:   Billy Goat One, what will you say?

Goat 1:   My fat little brother's coming this way!

Reader 2:   Billy Goat One just races along.

Reader 1:   Has no fear of that trip-trapping song.

Reader 2:   Little old troll, little old troll, what do you hear?

Troll: Another trip-trip-trapping coming near.

Reader 1:   Little old troll, little old troll, what will you do?

Troll: I'm still planning on having stew.

Readers Theatre: Scripted Rhymes and Rhythms   Braun & Braun ©

Reader 2:   Billy Goat Two, what do you hear?

Goat 2:   That same old troll is threatening me.

Reader 1:   Billy Goat Two, what will you say?

Goat 2:   There's one that's fatter heading this way.

Reader 2:   Billy Goat Two just trip-traps along,

Reader 1:   Closes his ears to that trip-trapping song.

Reader 2:   Little old troll, little old troll, what do you hear?

Troll: It must be the fat one trip-trapping near.

Reader 1:   Little old troll, little old troll, now what's your plan?

Troll: A yummy, chunky stew for me and Nan.

Reader 2:   Billy Goat Three, how do you feel?

Goat 3:   Those ugly, trolly threats, no big deal!

Reader 1:   But the ugly old troll is hungry, by Nilly,

Reader 2:   He's up on that bridge to catch this Billy.

Reader 1:   Billy Goat Three, I think you need help!

Goat 3:   No need, my friend, do you hear the yelp?

Reader 2:   Billy Goats, Billy Goats, what will you do?

3 Goats: There's grass enough for nice grassy stew.

THE THREE LITTLE PIGS

by Carl Braun

Reader 1:   The big bad wolf was out for a stroll,
What do you think he saw?

Voices: A rickety fence, a path in the meadow
Which led to a house of straw.

Reader 2:   The big bad wolf arrived at the house,
What do you think he did?

Voices: He huffed and he puffed, he puffed and he huffed,
And blew off the poor pig's lid.

Reader 3:   The big bad wolf continued his stroll,
What do you think he saw?

Voices: A pig in a fix in a house of sticks,
He jammed the door with his paw.

Readers Theatre: Scripted Rhymes and Rhythms

Reader 1:   The big bad wolf arrived at the house,
                  What do you think he found?

Voices: After huffing and puffing, and puffing and huffing,
                  A pig, and a house on the ground.

Reader 2:   The big bad wolf continued his stroll,
                  What do you think he heard?

Voices: A pig in a fix in a house of bricks,
                  A pig who had the last word.

Reader 3:   The big bad wolf arrived at the house,
                  What do you think he thought?

Voices: I'll huff and I'll puff, I'll puff and I'll huff,
                  And end that three-pig lot.

Readers 1, 2 and 3:   The big bad wolf was tired of huffing,
                       How does the story end?

Voices: He went home in a huff, no more puff,
                  The pigs had houses to mend.

CALICO PIE

by Edward Lear

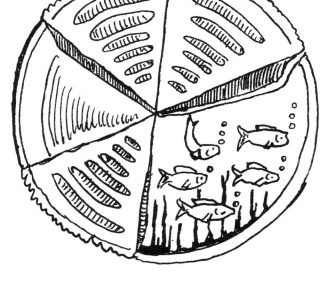

Reader 1: Calico Pie,
The little Birds fly
Down to the calico tree,

Reader 2: Their wings were blue,
And they sang,

Chorus: Tilly-loo!

Reader 3: Till away they flew —
And they never came back to me!

Chorus: They never came back!
They never came back!
They never came back to me!

Reader 1: Calico Jam,
The little Fish swam
Over the syllabub sea,

Reader 2: He took off his hat,
To the Sole and the Sprat,
And the Willeby-wat —

Reader 3: But he never came back to me!

Chorus: He never came back!

He never came back!

He never came back to me!

Reader 1: Calico Ban,

The little Mice ran,

To be ready in time for tea,

Reader 2: Flippity flup,

They drank it all up,

And danced in the cup —

Reader 3: But they never came back to me!

Chorus: They never came back!

They never came back!

They never came back to me!

Reader 1: Calico drum,

The Grasshoppers come,

The Butterfly, Beetle, and Bee,

Reader 2: Over the ground,

Around and round,

With a hop and a bound —

Reader 3: But they never came back!

All: They never came back!

They never came back!

They never came back to me!

THE DADDY LONG-LEGS AND THE FLY

by Edward Lear

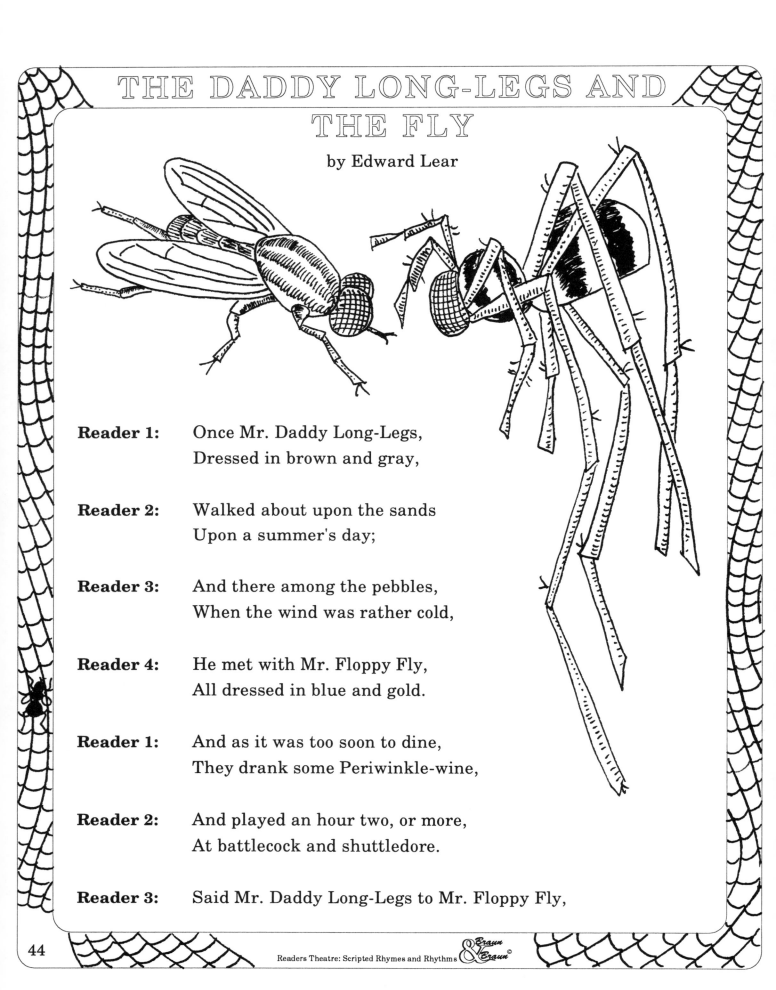

Reader 1:   Once Mr. Daddy Long-Legs,
                       Dressed in brown and gray,

Reader 2:   Walked about upon the sands
                       Upon a summer's day;

Reader 3:   And there among the pebbles,
                       When the wind was rather cold,

Reader 4:   He met with Mr. Floppy Fly,
                       All dressed in blue and gold.

Reader 1:   And as it was too soon to dine,
                       They drank some Periwinkle-wine,

Reader 2:   And played an hour two, or more,
                       At battlecock and shuttledore.

Reader 3:   Said Mr. Daddy Long-Legs to Mr. Floppy Fly,

Readers Theatre: Scripted Rhymes and Rhythms

Daddy Long-Legs: Why do you never come to court?
One in red, and one in green!
I wish you'd tell me why.
All gold and shine, in dress so fine,
You'd quite delight the court.
Why do you never go at all?
I really think you OUGHT!
And if you went, you'd see such sights!
Such rugs! and jugs! and candle-lights!
And more than all, the King and Queen,
One in red, and one in green!

Floppy Fly: O Mr. Daddy Long-Legs,

Reader 4: Said Mr. Floppy Fly,

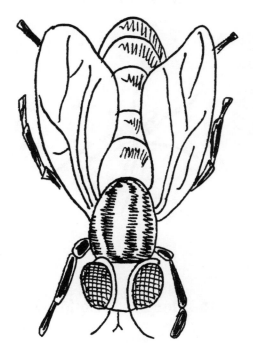

Floppy Fly: It's true I never go to court,
And I will tell you why.
If I had six long legs like yours,
At once I'd go to court!
But oh! I can't, because my legs
Are so extremely short.
And I'm afraid the King and Queen
(One in red, and one in green)
Would say aloud, 'You are not fit,
You Fly, to come to court a bit!'
O Mr. Daddy Long-Legs,

Reader 1: Said Mr. Floppy Fly,

Floppy Fly: I wish you'd sing one little song!
One mumbian melody!

You used to sing so awful well
In former days gone by,
But now you never sing at all;
I wish you'd tell me why:
For if you would, the silvery sound
Would please the shrimps and cockles round,
And all the crabs would gladly come
To hear you sing, 'Ah, Hum di Hum!'

Reader 2:   Said Mr. Daddy Long-Legs,

Daddy Long-Legs: I can never sing again!
And if you wish, I'll tell you why,
Although it gives me pain.
For years I could not hum a bit,
Or sing the smallest song;
And this the dreadful reason is,
My legs are grown too long!
My six long legs, all here and there,
Oppress my bosom with despair;
And if I stand, or lie, or sit,
I cannot sing one single bit!

Reader 3:   So Mr. Daddy Long-Legs
And Mr. Floppy Fly
Sat down in silence by the sea,
And gazed upon the sky.
They said,

Mr. D. Long-Legs & Mr. F. Fly: This is a dreadful thing!
The world has all gone wrong,

Since one has legs too short by half,
The other much too long!
One never more can go to court,
Because his legs have grown too short;
The other cannot sing a song,
Because his legs have grown too long!

Reader 4:   Then Mr. Daddy Long-Legs
And Mr. Floppy Fly
Rushed downward to the foaming sea
With one sponge-taneous cry;

Reader 1:   And there they found a little boat
Whose sails were pink and gray;
And off they sailed among the waves
Far, and far away.

Reader 2:   They sailed across the silent main
And reached the great Gromboolian plain;

Reader 3:   And there they play for evermore
At battlecock and shuttledore.

THE OWL AND THE PUSSY-CAT

by Edward Lear

Chorus 1:   The Owl and the Pussy-Cat went to sea

In a beautiful pea-green boat,

They took some honey, and plenty of money,

Wrapped up in a five-pound note.

Chorus 2:   The Owl looked up to the stars above,

And sang to a small guitar,

Owl: O lovely Pussy! O Pussy, my love,

What a beautiful Pussy you are,

Chorus 1:   You are,

You are!

What a beautiful Pussy you are!

Chorus 2:   Pussy said to the Owl,

Pussy: You elegant fowl!

How charmingly sweet you sing!

O let us be married! too long we have tarried:

Chorus 2:   But what shall we do for a ring?

Chorus 1:   So they sailed away for a year and a day,

To the land where the Bong-tree grows,

And there in a wood a Piggy-wig stood,

With a ring at the end of his nose,

Chorus 2:   His nose,

His nose,

With a ring at the end of his nose.

Owl & Pussy Cat: Dear Piggy, are you willing to sell for one shilling

Your ring?

Chorus 1:   Said the piggy,

Piggy: I will.

Chorus 2:   So they took it away, and were married the next day

By the Turkey who lives on the hill.

Chorus 1:   They dined upon mince, and slices of quince,

Which they ate with a runcible spoon;

Chorus 2:   And hand in hand, on the edge of the sand,

They danced by the light of the moon

Chorus 1 & 2:   The moon,

The moon,

They danced by the light of the moon.

THE DUCK AND THE KANGAROO

by Edward Lear

Reader 1:	Said the Duck to the Kangaroo,
Duck:	Good gracious! How you hop!
	Over the fields and the water too,
	As if you never would stop!
	My life is a bore in this nasty pond,
	And I long to go out in the world beyond!
	I wish I could hop like you!
Reader 2:	Said the Duck to the Kangaroo.
Duck:	Please give me a ride on your back!
Reader 1:	Said the Duck to the Kangaroo.
Duck:	I would sit quite still, and say nothing but Quack,
	The whole of the long day through!
	And we'd go to the Dee, and the Jelly Bo Lee,
	Over the land, and over the sea —
	Please take me a ride! O do!
Reader 2:	Said the Duck to the Kangaroo.
Reader 1:	Said the Kangaroo to the Duck,

Readers Theatre: Scripted Rhymes and Rhythms

Kangaroo: This requires some little reflection:

Perhaps on the whole it might bring me luck,

And there seems but one objection,

Which is, if you'll let me speak so bold,

Your feet are unpleasantly wet and cold,

And would probably give me the roo-

Matiz!

Reader 2: Said the Kangaroo.

Reader 1: Said the Duck,

Duck: As I sat on the rocks,

I have thought over that completely,

And I bought four pairs of worsted socks

Which fit my web-feet neatly.

And to keep out the cold I've bought a cloak,

And every day a cigar I'll smoke,

All to follow my own dear true

Love of a Kangaroo!

Reader 2: Said the Kangaroo,

Kangaroo: I'm ready!

All in the moonlight pale;

But to balance me well, dear Duck, sit steady!

And quite at the end of my tail!

Reader 1: So away they went with a hop and a bound,

Reader 2: And they hopped the whole world three times round;

Reader 1 & 2: And who so happy — O who,

As the Duck and the Kangaroo?

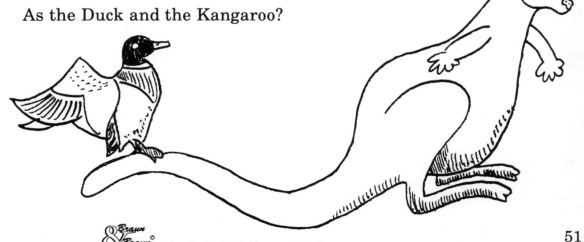

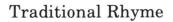
Traditional Rhyme

Reader 1: Mr. Finney had a turnip
And it grew and grew and grew,
Reader 2: It grew behind the barn,
Chorus: And the turnip did no harm.

Reader 1: And it grew, and it grew,
Till it could grow no taller,
Reader 2: And Mr. Finney took it
Chorus: And he put it in the cellar.

Reader 1: There it lay, there it lay,
Till it began to rot,
Reader 2: And his daughter Lizzie took it
Chorus: And she put it in the pot.

Reader 1: And she boiled it, and she boiled it,
As long as she was able,
Reader 2: And his daughter Susie took it
Chorus: And she put it on the table.

Reader 1: Mr. Finney and his wife
Both sat down to sup,
Reader 2: And they ate, and they ate,
Chorus: And they ate the turnip up!

THE ENORMOUS TURNIP AGAIN

by Carl Braun

Reader 1: A little old man planted some seeds,

Reader 2: He kept his garden free of weeds.

Reader 3: He could hardly believe his eyes,

When he noticed a turnip of pumpkin-size.

Reader 1: He went out to pull this enormous root,

Reader 2: He used his muscles from shoulder to boot.

Reader 3: It still wouldn't budge, so he let out a yelp,

Reader 1: Along came his wife to offer him help.

Reader 2: They pulled and they heaved to the count of three,

Reader 3: Still the giant veggie wouldn't go free.

Reader 1: The poor old couple, they gave all they had,

Reader 2: Then called for help from their young, little lad.

Reader 3:	With a heave and sigh and a Ho! Ho! Ho!
Reader 1:	The threesome made one curious show.
Reader 2:	They pulled and tugged without success,
Reader 3:	Then put out a call for their daughter, Bess.

Reader 1:	The turnip just clung to its roots in the earth,
Reader 2:	The foursome pulled for all they were worth.
Reader 3:	When they had worked every muscle there to be found,
	They put out a call for their spotted hound.

Reader 1:	The dog joined the four, gave all he could muster,
Reader 2:	The turnip, too large, even for Buster.
Reader 3:	They twisted, they turned, first this way, then that,
	Then joined in a chorus to invite kitty cat.

Reader 1:	Poor kitty just came from a mousing spree,
Reader 2:	But joined the pullsters with a one, two, three.
Reader 3:	She pulled and pulled with all her might,
Reader 1:	Then summoned a mouse who came in fright.

Reader 2:	The mouse put its weight to excellent use,
Reader 3:	The next thing you knew the turnip let loose.
Reader 1:	The gang fell over in a backwards bound,
Reader 2:	And lay for a minute in a strange-looking mound.

Reader 3:	But soon they were up, and scrubbed the big prize,
Reader 1:	And chopped it and cooked it for a village surprise.
Reader 2:	They added some pepper, some salt, and some leeks,
All:	The village had soup for the next two weeks.

Readers Theatre: Scripted Rhymes and Rhythms   Braun & Braun ©

Traditional

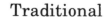

Reader 1:	The ants go marching one by one,
All:	*Hurrah! Hurrah!*
Reader 2:	The ants go marching one by one,
All:	*Hurrah! Hurrah!*
Reader 3:	The ants go marching one by one,
Reader 4:	The little one stopped to suck its thumb,
Reader 5:	And they all went marching down
	To the earth to get out of the rain,
All:	**BOOM! BOOM!**
	To the earth to get out of the rain.
Reader 1:	The ants go marching two by two,
All:	*Hurrah! Hurrah!*
Reader 2:	The ants go marching two by two,
All:	*Hurrah! Hurrah!*
Reader 3:	The ants go marching two by two,
Reader 4:	The little one stopped to do up its shoe,
Reader 5:	And they all went marching down
	To the earth to get out of the rain,
All:	**BOOM! BOOM!**
	To the earth to get out of the rain.

Reader 1: The ants go marching three by three,

All: *Hurrah! Hurrah!*

Reader 2: The ants go marching three by three,

All: *Hurrah! Hurrah!*

Reader 3: The ants go marching three by three,

Reader 4: The little one stopped to climb a tree,

Reader 5: And they all went marching down
To the earth to get out of the rain,

All: BOOM! BOOM!
To the earth to get out of the rain.

Reader 1: The ants go marching four by four,

All: *Hurrah! Hurrah!*

Reader 2: The ants go marching four by four,

All: *Hurrah! Hurrah!*

Reader 3: The ants go marching four by four,

Reader 4: The little one stopped to knock at the door,

Reader 5: And they all went marching down
To the earth to get out of the rain,

All: BOOM! BOOM!
To the earth to get out of the rain.

Reader 1: The ants go marching five by five,

All: *Hurrah! Hurrah!*

Reader 2: The ants go marching five by five,

All: *Hurrah! Hurrah!*

Reader 3: The ants go marching five by five,

Reader 4: The little one stopped to learn to drive,

Reader 5: And they all went marching down
To the earth to get out of the rain,

All: BOOM! BOOM!
To the earth to get out of the rain.

Readers Theatre: Scripted Rhymes and Rhythms

Reader 1: The ants go marching six by six,

All: *Hurrah! Hurrah!*

Reader 2: The ants go marching six by six,

All: *Hurrah! Hurrah!*

Reader 3: The ants go marching six by six,

Reader 4: The little one stopped to pick up sticks,

Reader 5: And they all went marching down

To the earth to get out of the rain,

All: **BOOM! BOOM!**

To the earth to get out of the rain.

Reader 1: The ants go marching seven by seven,

All: *Hurrah! Hurrah!*

Reader 2: The ants go marching seven by seven,

All: *Hurrah! Hurrah!*

Reader 3: The ants go marching seven by seven,

Reader 4: The little one stopped and went to heaven,

Reader 5: And they all went marching down

To the earth to get out of the rain,

All: **BOOM! BOOM!**

To the earth to get out of the rain.

Reader 1:   The ants go marching eight by eight,

All: *Hurrah! Hurrah!*

Reader 2:   The ants go marching eight by eight,

All: *Hurrah! Hurrah!*

Reader 3:   The ants go marching eight by eight,

Reader 4:   The little one stopped to shut the gate,

Reader 5:   And they all went marching down

To the earth to get out of the rain,

All: **BOOM! BOOM!**

To the earth to get out of the rain.

Reader 1:   The ants go marching nine by nine,

All: *Hurrah! Hurrah!*

Reader 2:   The ants go marching nine by nine,

All: *Hurrah! Hurrah!*

Reader 3:   The ants go marching nine by nine,

Reader 4:   The little one stopped to walk on a line,

Reader 5:   And they all went marching down

To the earth to get out of the rain,

All: **BOOM! BOOM!**

To the earth to get out of the rain.

Reader 1:   The ants go marching ten by ten,

All: *Hurrah! Hurrah!*

Reader 2:   The ants go marching ten by ten,

All: *Hurrah! Hurrah!*

Reader 3:   The ants go marching ten by ten,

Reader 4:   The little one stopped to say . . .

All: **THE END!**

MOTHER DOESN'T WANT A DOG

by Judith Viorst

Reader 1:   Mother doesn't want a dog.
                        Mother says they smell.
                        And never sit when you say sit,
Reader 2:   Or even when you yell.
Reader 3:   And when you come home late at night
                        And there is ice and snow,
                        You have to go back out because
                        The dumb dog has to go.

Reader 1:   Mother doesn't want a dog.
Reader 2:   Mother says they shed,
Reader 3:   And always let the strangers in
                        And bark at friends instead,
Reader 1:   And do disgraceful things on rugs,
Reader 2:   And track mud on the floor,
Reader 3:   And flop upon your bed at night
                        And snore their doggy snore.

Reader 1:   Mother doesn't want a dog.
All: She's making a mistake.
                        Because, more than a dog, I think
                        She will not want this snake.

OVER IN THE MEADOW

Traditional

Reader 1:   Over in the meadow
                   In the sand in the sun
Reader 2:   Lived an old mother turtle
Reader 3:   And her little turtle one.
Reader 4:   "Dig," said the mother.
All: "I dig," said the one.
Reader 5:   So they dug all day
                   In the sand in the sun.

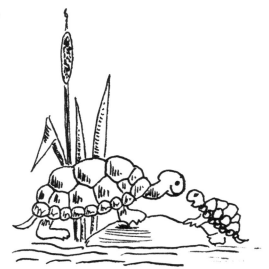

Reader 1:   Over in the meadow
                   Where the stream runs blue
Reader 2:   Lived an old mother fish
Reader 3:   And her little fishes two.
Reader 4:   "Swim," said the mother.
All: "We swim," said the two.
Reader 5:   So they swam all day
                   Where the stream runs blue.

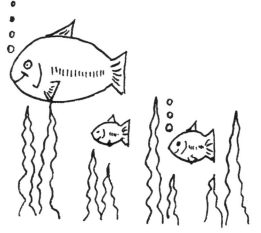

Reader 1:   Over in the meadow
                   In a hole in a tree
Reader 2:   Lived an old mother owl
Reader 3:   And her little owls three.
Reader 4:   "Tu-whoo," said the mother.
All: "We tu-whoo," said the three.
Reader 5:   So they tu-whoo'd all night
                   In a hole in a tree.

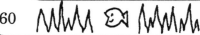

Readers Theatre: Scripted Rhymes and Rhythms Braun & Braun

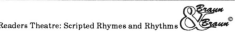

Reader 1:	Over in the meadow
	By an old barn door
Reader 2:	Lived an old mother mouse
Reader 3:	And her little mice four.
Reader 4:	"Gnaw," said the mother.
All:	"We gnaw," said the four.
Reader 5:	So they gnawed all day
	By the old barn door.

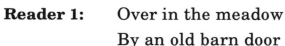

Reader 1:	Over in the meadow
	In a sunny beehive
Reader 2:	Lived an old mother bee
Reader 3:	And her little bees five.
Reader 4:	"Buzz," said the mother.
All:	"We buzz," said the five.
Reader 5:	So they buzzed all day
	In a sunny beehive.

Reader 1:	Over in the meadow
	In a nest made of sticks
Reader 2:	Lived an old mother crow
Reader 3:	And her little crows six.
Reader 4:	"Caw," said the mother.
All:	"We caw," said the six.
Reader 5:	So they cawed all day
	In a nest made of sticks.

Reader 1:	Over in the meadow
	Where the grass grows even
Reader 2:	Lived an old mother frog
Reader 3:	And her little frogs seven.
Reader 4:	"Jump," said the mother.
All:	"We jump," said the seven.
Reader 5:	So they jumped all day
	Where the grass grows even.

Reader 1:	Over in the meadow
	By the old mossy gate
Reader 2:	Lived an old mother lizard
Reader 3:	And her little lizards eight.
Reader 4:	"Bask," said the mother.
All:	"We bask," said the eight.
Reader 5:	So they basked all day
	By the old mossy gate.

62

Reader 1: Over in the meadow
By the old Scotch pine
Reader 2: Lived an old mother duck
Reader 3: And her little ducklings nine.
Reader 4: "Quack," said the mother.
All: "We quack," said the nine.
Reader 5: So they quacked all day
By the old Scotch pine.

Reader 1: Over in the meadow
In a cozy wee den
Reader 2: Lived an old mother beaver
Reader 3: And her little beavers ten.
Reader 4: "Beave," said the mother.
All: "We beave," said the ten.
Reader 5: So they beaved all day
In the cozy wee den.

OVER IN THE ZOO

by Carl Braun

Reader 1: Over in the zoo
When the day is done,
Reader 2: Lives an old mother dove
Reader 3: And her little dove one.
Reader 4: "Coo," says the mother,
Reader 5: "I coo," says the one,
Reader 6: So it coos and coos
Reader 7: When the day is done.

Reader 1: Over in the zoo
In an old tattered shoe,
Reader 2: Lives an old mother mouse,
Reader 3: And her little mice two.
Reader 4: "Squeak," says the mother,
Readers 5 & 6: "We squeak," say the two,
Reader 7: So they squeak all day,
Reader 1: In that old tattered shoe.

Reader 2: Over in the zoo,
In an old cherry tree,
Reader 3: Lives an old mother bee,
Reader 4: And her little bees three.
Reader 5: "Buzz," says the mother,
1, 2 & 3: "We buzz," say the three,
Reader 6: So they buzz all day
Reader 7: In the old cherry tree.

Readers Theatre: Scripted Rhymes and Rhythms   Braun & Braun©

Reader 1:	Over in the zoo,
	Near the ice-cream store,
Reader 2:	Lives an old mother bear,
Reader 3:	And her little cubs four.
Reader 1:	"Sniff," says the mother,
4, 5, 6 & 7:	"Sniff, sniff," go the four,
Reader 2:	So they sniff all day
Reader 3:	Near the ice-cream store.

Reader 4:	Over in the zoo,
	Where the ducklings dive,
Reader 5:	Lives an old mother goose,
Reader 6:	And her little goslings five.
Reader 7:	"Honk," says the mother,
All:	"Honk, honk," say the five,
Reader 1:	So they honk all day
Reader 2:	Where the ducklings dive.

Reader 3:	Over in the zoo
	In a house of bricks,
Reader 4:	Lives an old mother tiger,
Reader 5:	And her little cubs six.
Reader 6:	"Grrrr," says the mother,
All:	"Grrrr, Grrrr," say the six,
Reader 7:	So they Grrrr all day
Reader 1:	In a house made of bricks.

Reader 2: Over in the zoo,
At the stroke of eleven,
Reader 3: Calls an old zookeeper
Reader 4: To a monkey clan of seven.
Reader 5: "Eat," says the keeper,
All: "We eat," say the seven,
Reader 6: So they eat and they eat
Reader 7: At the stroke of eleven.

Reader 1: Over in the zoo
Free of hooks and bait,
Reader 2: Lives an old mother sunfish,
Reader 3: And her little sunfish eight.
Reader 4: "Swim," says the mother,
All: "We swim," say the eight,
Reader 5: So they swim all day,
Reader 6: Free of hooks and bait.

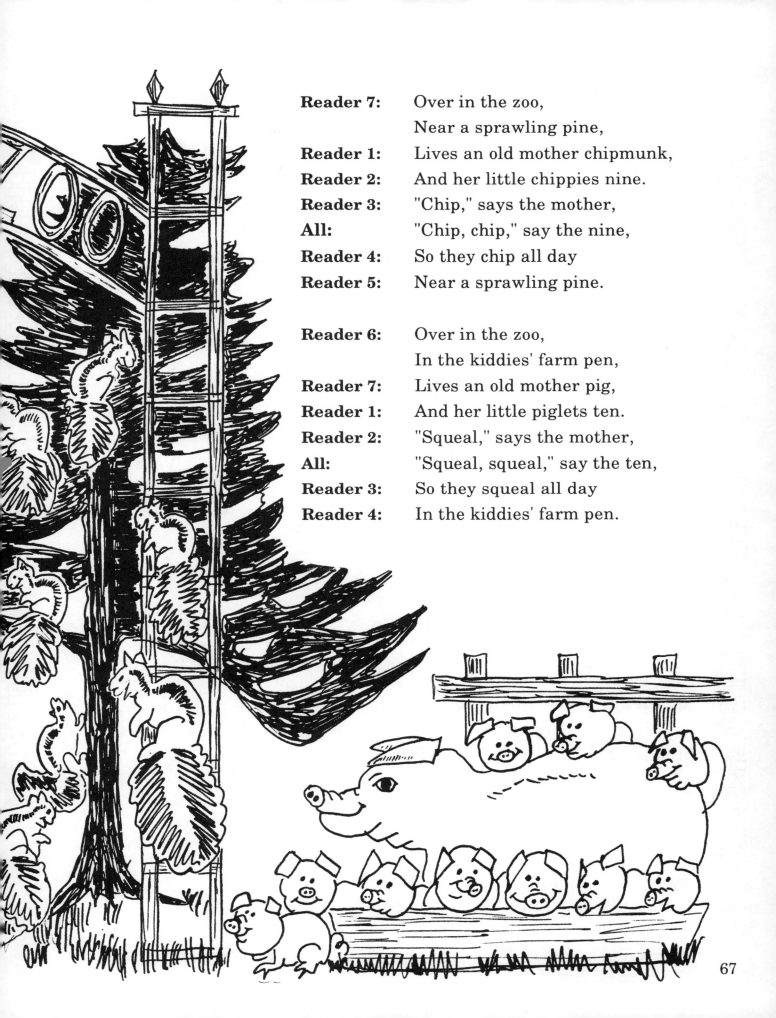

Reader 7: Over in the zoo,
Near a sprawling pine,
Reader 1: Lives an old mother chipmunk,
Reader 2: And her little chippies nine.
Reader 3: "Chip," says the mother,
All: "Chip, chip," say the nine,
Reader 4: So they chip all day
Reader 5: Near a sprawling pine.

Reader 6: Over in the zoo,
In the kiddies' farm pen,
Reader 7: Lives an old mother pig,
Reader 1: And her little piglets ten.
Reader 2: "Squeal," says the mother,
All: "Squeal, squeal," say the ten,
Reader 3: So they squeal all day
Reader 4: In the kiddies' farm pen.

TOPSY-TURVEY ZOO

by Helen G. Hall

Reader 1: Mother, mother
Come to the zoo
Reader 2: A monkey has swallowed
The kangaroo.

Reader 1: A lion is chasing
The circus clown;
Reader 2: The tigers are running
Upside down.

Reader 1: The turtles are taking
The bears for a ride,
Reader 2: The zebras have fun
On a slippery slide.

Reader 1: They're sliding down
The tall giraffe,
Reader 2: Mother, mother
It will make you laugh.

Readers Theatre: Scripted Rhymes and Rhythms

ABOUT THE AUTHORS

Carl Braun, Ph.D, LL.D, a past president of the International Reading Association is Professor Emeritus of Educational Psychology at the University of Calgary. He has taught children in elementary and secondary classrooms in both urban and rural schools. He continues to work with children and conducts workshops on assessment and instructional strategies. He loves reading to, and with children, especially his seven grandchildren. His favourite pastime: responding to the exhortation, "Read it again, Pops."

Win Braun, B.Ed., has taught all levels from grade one to grade six in Alberta. She spent two years teaching English at West China Medical University and Luzhou Medical College in China. She is currently at home with her two small children, Tyler and Mikala, who share her love of books.

ABOUT THE ILLUSTRATOR

Jeff Reading, BA, B.Ed., MA, is a teacher and consultant in Environmental and Outdoor Education in Calgary. He has worked with all grades and is presently teaching elementary school science. He enjoys spending time outdoors with his wife Shelagh and their two children, David and Meghan.